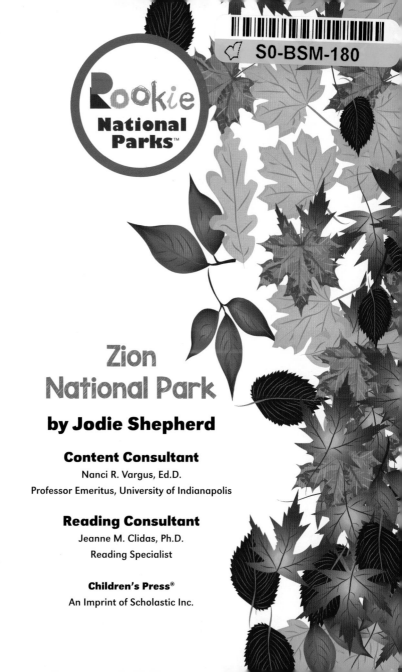

Rookie
National Parks™

Zion
National Park

by Jodie Shepherd

Content Consultant

Nanci R. Vargus, Ed.D.
Professor Emeritus, University of Indianapolis

Reading Consultant

Jeanne M. Clidas, Ph.D.
Reading Specialist

Children's Press®
An Imprint of Scholastic Inc.

Library of Congress Cataloging-in-Publication Data
Names: Shepherd, Jodie, author.
Title: Zion National Park/by Jodie Shepherd (content consultant), Nanci R. Vargus, Ed.D. (reading consultant), Jeanne M. Clidas, Ph.D. (reading specialist).
Description: New York: Children's Press, an imprint of Scholastic Inc., 2018. | Series: Rookie national parks | Includes index.
Identifiers: LCCN 2016057410| ISBN 9780531233368 (library binding) | ISBN 9780531239087 (paperback)
Subjects: LCSH: Zion National Park (Utah)—Juvenile literature. | Vargus, Nanci Reginelli, reading consultant. | Clidas, Jeanne, reading specialist.
Classification: LCC F832.Z8 S36 2018 | DDC 979.2/48—dc23
LC record available at https://lccn.loc.gov/2016057410

Produced by Spooky Cheetah Press
Design: Judith Christ-Lafond/Brenda Jackson/Joan Michael

Published in 2018 by Children's Press, an imprint of Scholastic Inc., 557 Broadway, New York, NY 10012.

Printed in China 62

SCHOLASTIC, CHILDREN'S PRESS, ROOKIE NATIONAL PARKS™, and associated logos are trademarks and/or registered trademarks of Scholastic Inc.

1 2 3 4 5 6 7 8 9 10 R 27 26 25 24 23 22 21 20 19 18

Photographs ©: cover: Matt Anderson Photography/Getty Images; back cover: Arpad Benedek/iStockphoto; 1-2: PCRex/Shutterstock; 3: GeorgeBurba/iStockphoto; 4-5: theasis/iStockphoto; 6: David Epperson/Getty Images; 7: OLOS/Shutterstock; 8-9: David Wall/Alamy Images; 9 inset: Dennis Frates/Alamy Images; 10-11: Witold Skrypczak/Getty Images; 10 inset: World-Travel/Thinkstock; 12: sandiegoa/iStockphoto; 13: Anthony Heflin/Shutterstock; 14 main: Niebrugge Images/Alamy Images; 14 inset: Visual&Written/Newscom; 15: Andrew Turner/Flickr; 16-17: S Sailer/A Sailer/age fotostock; 17 inset: Sloot/iStockphoto; 18-19: Caleb Weston/EyeEm/Getty Images; 18 top inset: Pritz Pritz/Getty Images; 18 bottom inset: ZionNPS/Flickr; 20 main: Mpetroff/Dreamstime; 20 inset: kenowolfpack/Thinkstock; 21: Craig K Lorenz/Getty Images; 22-23: Nancybelle Gonzaga Villarroya/Getty Images; 22 left inset: Carrie Davis/Dreamstime; 22 right inset: Steven Love/Dreamstime; 24-25: Stephanie Lupoli/Shutterstock; 25 top inset: Russ Bishop/Alamy Images; 25 bottom inset: athertoncustoms/iStockphoto; 26-27 background: DavidMSchrader/iStockphoto; 26 top left: Josef Pittner/Shutterstock; 26 top center: Irina Kozhemyakina/Dreamstime; 26 top right: Davies and Starr/Getty Images; 26 bottom left: Konstantin Shevtsov/Dreamstime; 26 bottom center: mallardg500/Getty Images; 26 bottom right: Steve Johnson/Getty Images; 27 top left: Joel Sartore/Getty Images; 27 top right: reptiles4all/Shutterstock; 27 bottom left: Michael E Halstead/Shutterstock; 27 bottom center: Roman Spoutil/Shutterstock; 27 bottom right: GlobalP/iStockphoto; 30 A: Daniela Duncan/Getty Images; 30 B: JeffGoulden/iStockphoto; 30 C: John Cancalosi/Getty Images; 30 D: Dan Leeth/Alamy Images; 31 top: theasis/iStockphoto; 31 center top: sandiegoa/iStockphoto; 31 center bottom: Witold Skrypczak/Getty Images; 31 bottom: James Marvin Phelps/Shutterstock; 32: James O'Neil/Getty Images.

Maps by Jim McMahon.

Table of Contents

I am Ranger Red Fox, your tour guide. Are you ready for an amazing adventure in Zion?

Welcome to Zion National Park!

Zion is in southern Utah. It was made a **national park** in 1919. People visit national parks to explore nature.

The word *zion* means "safe, peaceful place." The park is filled with beautiful **canyons**. It is home to incredible animals and plants.

These layers
of rock
formed
over millions
of years.

American Indians called this place Mukuntuweap (**mew**-ken-chew-ap). That means "straight-up canyon." Visitors to Zion stand at the bottom of the canyon. They look up at the steep, orange- and red-colored cliffs. The view is amazing!

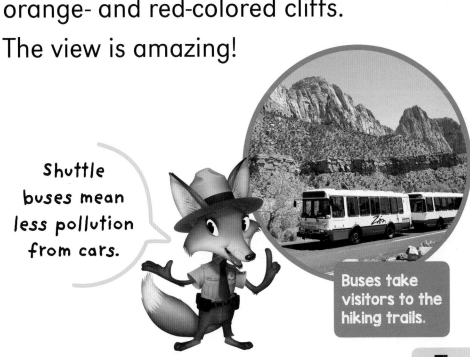

Shuttle buses mean less pollution from cars.

Buses take visitors to the hiking trails.

Chapter 1

Rock the Park

Zion did not always look this way. About 250 million years ago, the area was covered by a shallow sea. Over millions of years, the sea became lakes. Then the area turned into desert. Forces under the earth pushed up huge sandstone cliffs.

The land is still changing. Year after year, wind and water reshape the cliffs.

This steep zigzag trail is called Walter's Wiggles. At the top, hikers get a stunning view from Angels Landing.

If you take your car to the park, you can drive right through the cliffs! The Zion-Mount Carmel Tunnel opened in 1930. The tunnel is famous. It was hard to dig a road through the rock.

The tunnel is about a mile long. It took three years to build.

There are six windows carved into the tunnel. They let in light and fresh air. They also let in amazing views! Just outside the tunnel, visitors pass Checkerboard **Mesa**.

Look at the photo. Can you guess how Checkerboard Mesa got its name?

Many visitors stop their cars to get a good look at this unique rock formation.

Chapter 2

Let It Grow!

Some parts of Zion are high and others low. So there are many **habitats**. There are desert areas and woodlands. Wetlands line the riverbanks.

Each habitat is home to different types of trees and plants. These range from desert cacti to the pine trees that grow in the park's highest spots.

Ponderosa pines

Watch out for the sharp spines of the cacti. Yow!

The prickly pear cactus grows in the lower parts of the park.

13

Golden columbines grow in the hanging gardens.

Water seeps through the rocks, allowing the plants to grow there.

In Zion's famous "hanging gardens," plants seem to grow straight out of the rocks. The gardens are home to many unique plants. They are also home to the world's smallest snail. The Zion snail looks like a tiny black spot on the rocky cliffs.

This tiny creature can be found only in this park.

Zion snail

Chapter 3

Watch Out for Water!

Much of Zion is desert. But water is still an important part of the park. Animals need the water to live.

The Virgin River and smaller streams that empty into it wind through the park. A trail called the Narrows leads hikers along the river at the bottom of the canyon.

Want to hike the Narrows? You will have to get your feet wet!

Flash floods are a danger! They happen when heavy rainfall causes the river's water level to rise suddenly.

Rainfall and melting snow become rushing water.

Kolob Arch is one of the largest natural arches in the world.

The part of the park known as Kolob Canyons gets more rain than the rest of Zion. Spring rains bring beautiful waterfalls to this quiet area.

The skies over Zion are very dark at night. That makes the stargazing out of this world!

California condor

Bighorn sheep scamper on Zion's cliffs.

The endangered California condor is the largest bird in North America.

20

Chapter 4

Wonderful Wildlife

Zion is home to all kinds of animals. Some are endangered. That means few are left. Desert bighorn sheep had disappeared from Zion completely. Then scientists brought some back to the park. Now there are more than 400!

Mexican spotted owl

Mule deer are easy to spot in the park. They get their name from their large mule-like ears. Their sense of smell is about one thousand times as good as a person's!

giant desert hairy scorpion

desert tarantula

Tarantulas are not dangerous to humans, but watch out for a scorpion's sting!

A mule deer baby, or fawn, has a spotted coat for the first few months of its life.

Visitors explore Zion National Park in lots of ways. They may ride horses or bicycles. They may go rock climbing or hiking. Any way you choose, this park is always a wild adventure!

Imagine you could visit Zion. What would you do there?

Kids enjoy nature in many ways at Zion!

EMERALD POOLS TRAIL
o UPPER POOL   1.5 MILE o
o MIDDLE POOL   1.0 MILE o
o LOWER POOL   0.6 MILE o
o SAND BENCH TRAIL o

SLIPPERY WHEN
WET OR ICY

These are just some of the incredible animals that make their home in Zion.

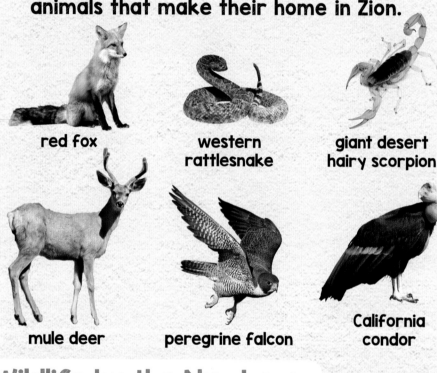

red fox

western rattlesnake

giant desert hairy scorpion

mule deer

peregrine falcon

California condor

Wildlife by the Numbers
The park is home to about...

291 types of birds **78** types of mammals

If you're lucky, you may see me or my cousin, the gray fox, in Zion!

Mexican spotted owl

horned leopard lizard

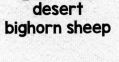

desert bighorn sheep

canyon tree frog

mountain lion

44 types of reptiles and amphibians

8 types of fish

Where Is Ranger Red Fox?

Oh no! Ranger Red Fox has lost his way in the park. But you can help. Use the map and the clues below to find him.

1. Ranger Red Fox started at an orange arch in Kolob Canyons.

2. Then he walked southeast to the Narrows. It felt good to cool off in the river on a hot day!

3. Next, he walked south and started up a zigzag path to Angels Landing. He got dizzy and had to turn around!

4. Finally, he went south again. He found a long, cool tunnel to protect him from the heat.

Help! Can you find me?

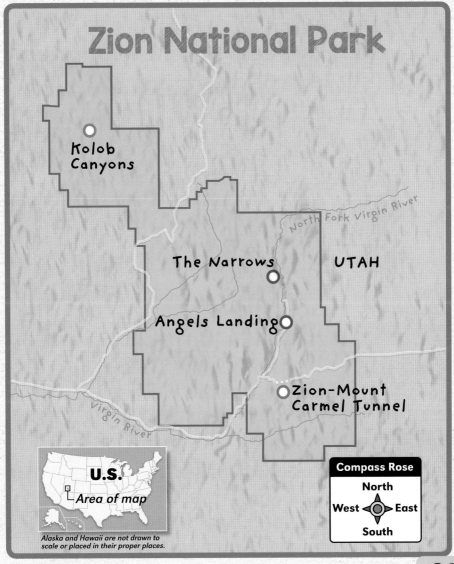

Zion National Park

Kolob Canyons

North Fork Virgin River

The Narrows

UTAH

Angels Landing

Zion–Mount Carmel Tunnel

Virgin River

U.S.
Area of map

Alaska and Hawaii are not drawn to scale or placed in their proper places.

Compass Rose

North

West — East

South

Wildflower Tracker

Can you match each wildflower to its name? Read the clues to help you.

A.

B.

D.

C.

1. Slickrock paintbrush
Clue: This plant has spiky, bright red petals.

2. Sacred datura
Clue: This big white bloom opens at night, when the air is cooler.

3. Prickly pear cactus
Clue: This plant's pretty flowers grow between sharp, pointy spines.

4. Golden columbine
Clue: This flower's name tells you its color. It grows in Zion's hanging gardens.

30

Answers: 1. D; 2. C; 3. B; 4. A

Glossary

canyons (**kan**-yuhns): deep, narrow river valleys with steep sides

habitats (**hab**-i-tats): places where animals or plants are usually found

mesa (**may**-suh): large hill with steep sides and a flat top

national park (**nash**-uh-nuhl pahrk): area where the land and its animals are protected by the U.S. government

Index

Facts for Now

Visit this Scholastic Web site for more information on Zion National Park:

www.factsfornow.scholastic.com

Enter the keyword **Zion**

About the Author

Jodie Shepherd, who also writes under her real name, Leslie Kimmelman, is the award-winning author of dozens of fiction and nonfiction titles for children. She is also a children's book editor. Jodie recently visited Zion National Park and thought it was absolutely spectacular.